Voting for President

Sherry Howard, M.Ed.

Reader Consultants

Brian Allman, M.A.
Classroom Teacher, West Virginia

Cynthia Donovan
Classroom Teacher, California

iCivics Consultants

Emma Humphries, Ph.D.
Chief Education Officer

Taylor Davis, M.T.
Director of Curriculum and Content

Natacha Scott, MAT
Director of Educator Engagement

Contributing Author: Dani Neiley

Publishing Credits

Rachelle Cracchiolo, M.S.Ed., *Publisher*
Emily R. Smith, M.A.Ed., *VP of Content Development*
Véronique Bos, *Creative Director*
Dona Herweck Rice, *Senior Content Manager*
Dani Neiley, *Associate Editor*
Fabiola Sepulveda, *Series Designer*

Image Credits: p4 Alamy/Abaca Press; p5 Shutterstock/Christopher Penler; p10 Library of Congress [LC-USZ62-995]; p11 Virginia Museum of Fine Arts; p13 Shutterstock/Everett Collection; p14 top Shutterstock/Jeremy Bustin Photography; p14 bottom Shutterstock/Gino Santa Maria; p17 Alamy/Reuters; p18 Alamy Stock Photo; p19 Shutterstock/Rosamar; pp20–21 Alamy Stock Photo; p21 top Shutterstock/Aarchna Nautiyal; p22 Alamy/Reuters; p23 Shutterstock/Sundry Photography; p24 Alamy/Stock Connection Blue; p25 Alamy/Jeffrey Isaac Greenberg 13+; p27 AFP via Getty Images; p28 Alamy Stock Photo; p29 Shutterstock/Joseph Sohm; all other images from iStock and/or Shutterstock

Library of Congress Cataloging-in-Publication Data

Names: Howard, Sherry, author.
Title: Voting for president / Sherry Howard.
Other titles: ICivics (Teacher Created Materials, Inc.)
Description: Huntington Beach, CA : Teacher Created Materials, [2022] | Includes index. | Audience: Grades 4-6 | Summary: "Electing a president is a key right and responsibility of being a U.S. citizen. The process for choosing the next leader can seem complex. It is important to understand how presidential elections work so that people can be informed voters. Learn more about how Americans choose a president and why every vote matters"-- Provided by publisher.
Identifiers: LCCN 2021045431 (print) | LCCN 2021045432 (ebook) | ISBN 9781087607153 (Paperback) | ISBN 9781087628776 (ePub)
Subjects: LCSH: Presidents--United States--Election--Juvenile literature.
Classification: LCC JK528 .H69 2022 (print) | LCC JK528 (ebook) | DDC 324.973--dc23/eng/20211102
LC record available at https://lccn.loc.gov/2021045431
LC ebook record available at https://lccn.loc.gov/2021045432

TCM | Teacher Created Materials

5482 Argosy Avenue
Huntington Beach, CA 92649
www.tcmpub.com

ISBN 978-1-0876-0715-3

Table of Contents

Choosing a President

Choosing the president of the United States is a big responsibility. The president is the most powerful single leader in the country. **Citizens** of the United States vote for their leaders. They choose the people they think will do the best jobs. Ideally, they give their votes a lot of thought. They make careful decisions.

The system of electing the president has been in place for hundreds of years. At first look, it may seem complicated. But the early leaders had strong reasons for designing the process as they did. The process has several steps. Every election cycle, those steps are followed.

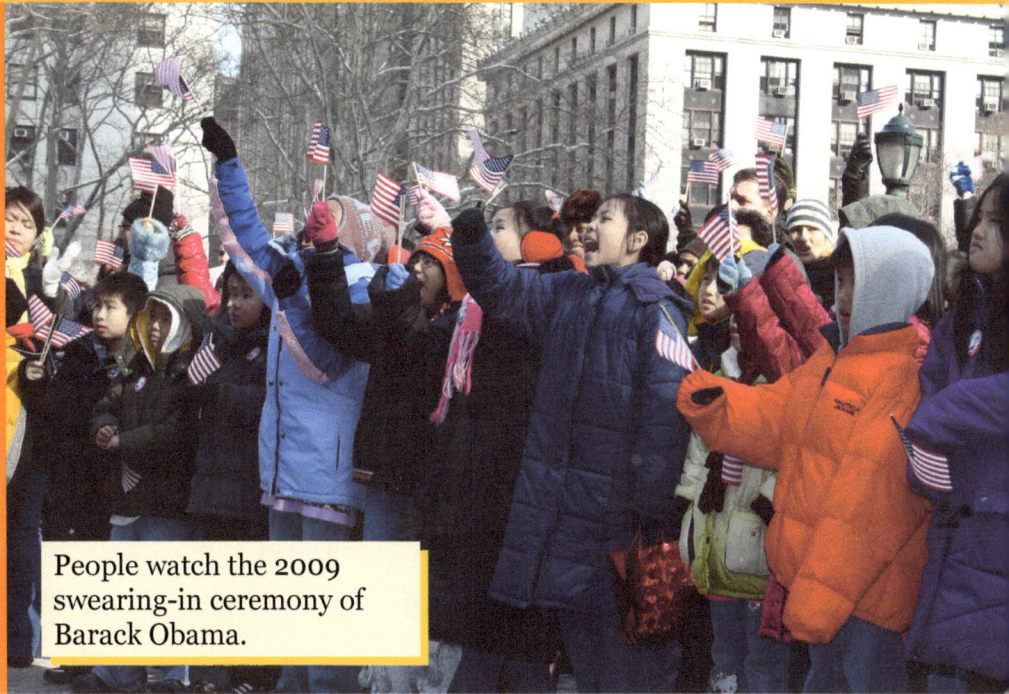

People watch the 2009 swearing-in ceremony of Barack Obama.

Most U.S. citizens are allowed to vote when they turn 18. But whether they are old enough to vote or not, they can and should stay informed about what the president does. The president represents the country. Even if a person cannot vote, they can still be involved. They can write letters to leaders. They can show support for **candidates** and ideas.

It is good when the public stays involved in politics. People should know how the election process works. This helps them make the most of their voices and their votes. In a **democracy**, the people are the true leaders, and the president works for them!

Jump into Fiction

Letters ^{to} Leaders

Maria sighed. Randall had kicked the ball and missed the net. But that wasn't what upset Maria. The soccer field at school was all dirt. When people missed the net, the ball just rolled and rolled. Most of Maria's recess was spent chasing down the ball. She took a deep breath and began to run...again!

After recess, a tired Maria slumped back to class and dropped into her chair. When she glanced up at the board, she saw that Mrs. Rodriguez had written "Letters to Leaders."

"Okay, class, please get out your writing journals and pencils," Mrs. Rodriguez began. "Today, we are going to write letters to our student council members. They would like our students to explain what they think are the biggest problems facing the school. Then, the student council will work to fix those problems throughout the year."

Maria perked up. Normally, writing was her least favorite subject. She would much rather spend twice the amount of time on math and avoid writing altogether. But today, she was inspired. She knew exactly what problem should be fixed.

"Dear Student Council," Maria wrote. "The soccer field needs grass. I spend most of my recess chasing the soccer ball as it rolls across the dirt. It is hard work! It can also be dangerous. Last week, Lydia slid in the dirt and hit her head! Having grass on the field will help the players and the game!"

Maria reread her letter. She thought it sounded good. She had explained the problem and how it affected students. Maria handed her letter to Mrs. Rodriguez.

Dear Student Council,

The following week, the student council president, Kristina, came in to see Maria's class. Kristina said a lot of students had written about wanting more posters in the lunchroom. Kristina also said that people wanted the student council store to stay open longer after school. Maria frowned. It looked like her idea wasn't going to be mentioned.

"Finally," Kristina continued, "we had a request for grass on the soccer field. We needed the school's help with that one. Principal Barnes took the issue to the PTA. They voted to help us buy grass seed. Thanks to Maria for her letter!"

Kristina smiled at Maria while her class started to clap. Maria grinned and cheered. Her letter worked!

Back to Nonfiction

Early Steps for a New Nation

Many years ago, the early leaders of the country wrote the Constitution. In it, the writers, or **Framers**, described how people would choose their leaders. The United States had just fought a war to earn its independence. Before the war, one king ruled the nation. The people did not have a say in what was done. So, the Framers wanted to do things differently. They did not want a king or queen telling the people what to do.

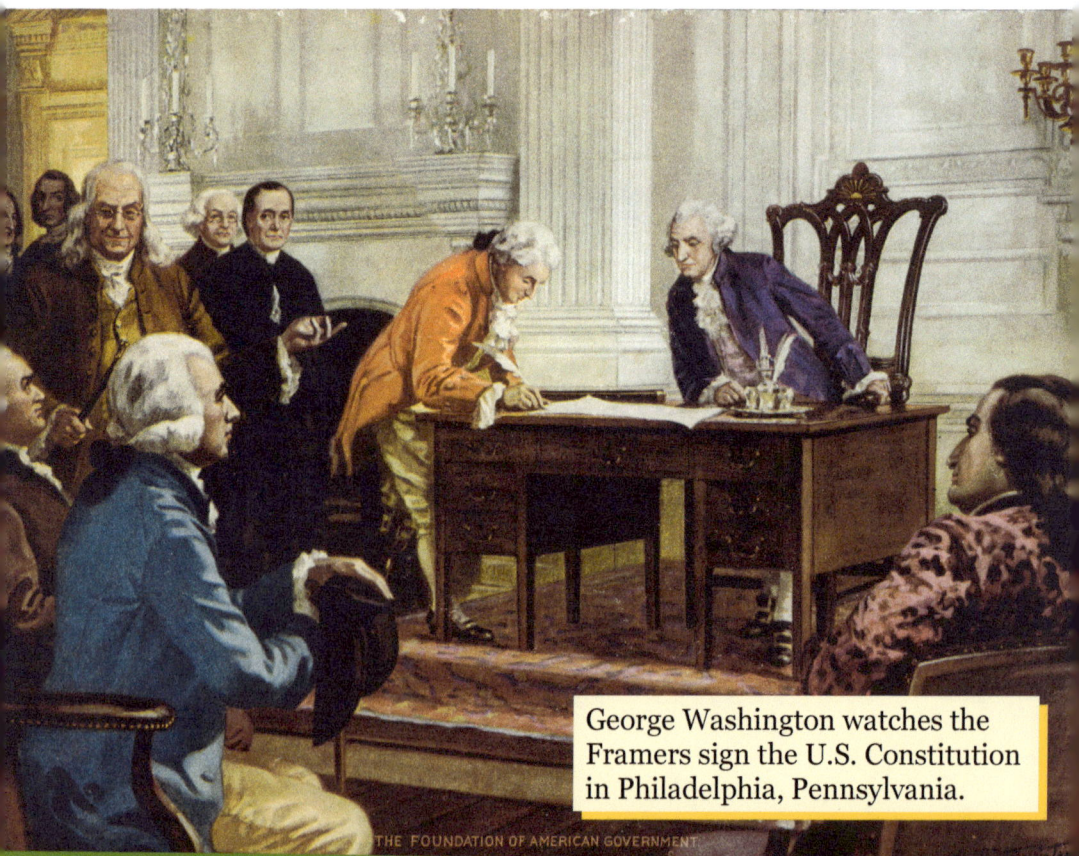

George Washington watches the Framers sign the U.S. Constitution in Philadelphia, Pennsylvania.

THE FOUNDATION OF AMERICAN GOVERNMENT

Constitutional Convention

The Framers met at the Constitutional Convention. At these meetings, they discussed how they wanted to change the country's government. They met together for just under four months, from May 25 to September 17, 1787.

Some Framers wanted Congress to choose a leader. Some Framers wanted a **popular vote** so all voters had a chance to choose. People had strong opinions on both sides. They argued for months over the best way to choose leaders. Finally, in 1787, the Framers worked out a **compromise**. The people of the nation would vote. Then, the Electoral College would choose the winner. This was a way to balance what the Framers wanted. They would not have to choose between Congress and the popular vote. The new nation would rely on both.

Early leaders predicted the growth the United States would have. They thought about possible problems. So, the Constitution allows for changes. The changes are called **amendments**.

A few amendments have focused on voting rights. At first, only certain men were allowed to vote. The men had to be white and had to own land. They had to be over the age of 21. That meant a lot of people could not legally vote. People of color and women were all **excluded**.

Most people knew that this was not fair. The nation could not be a true democracy if large groups of people could not vote for their leaders. Over time, more and more groups of people gained the right to vote. Amendments to the Constitution allowed for these changes. Amendments made it so that people could vote regardless of how wealthy they were, the color of their skin, or their gender.

National League of Women Voters in 1924

President Ulysses S. Grant signs the Fifteenth Amendment.

People have had to work hard to make sure that all citizens have the legal right to vote. It is now both a right and a responsibility of U.S. citizens. And people still work to protect this right.

Expanding Voting Rights

Black men gained the legal right to vote in 1870. This right was granted through the Fifteenth Amendment. The Nineteenth Amendment was passed in 1920. That gave women the legal right to vote.

Candidates and Parties

Today, most U.S. citizens who are 18 or older can vote. But not every citizen can become president. There are three rules for who can become president. First, the person has to be a natural-born citizen. This means they must be a U.S. citizen at their birth. A person who is born in a different country can be president as long as their parents are U.S. citizens. Second, the person must be at least 35 years old. Finally, the person must have lived in the United States for at least 14 years. Candidates who meet these requirements can run for president.

Hillary Clinton was a Democratic candidate.

John McCain was a Republican candidate.

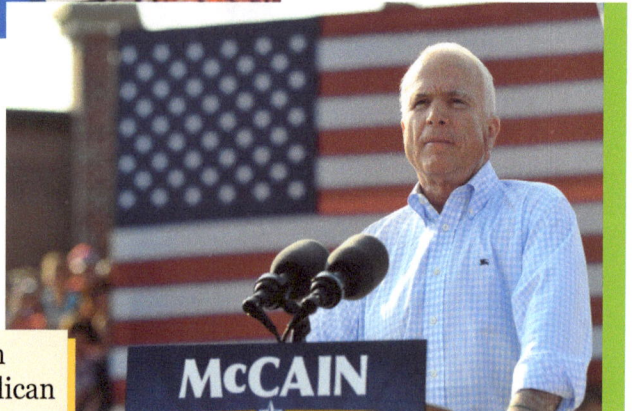

A Long Job

Presidents serve four-year terms. They can be elected twice, meaning they can serve eight years total. Presidential elections are held every four years. Election Day is always on the Tuesday after the first Monday in November.

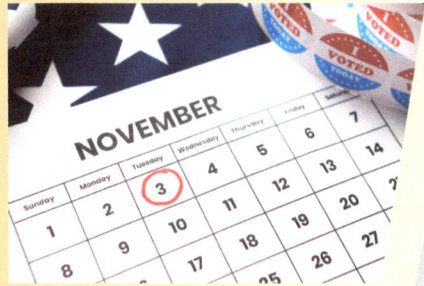

Each presidential candidate usually belongs to a **political party**. There are two main parties in the United States. But, there is no rule about how many parties there can be. The two main parties today are the Republican Party and the Democratic Party. These are not the only two options. There are also many smaller parties. The Green Party and the Libertarian Party are just two examples. People do not have to join any of these parties. You can be an independent. This means you do not belong to any party at all.

The Start of the Process

The first step in the election process happens when a candidate announces they plan to run for president. This usually happens about two years before Election Day. This is when their **campaign** officially begins.

Think and Talk

Why do you think it is important for campaigns to start nearly two years before Election Day?

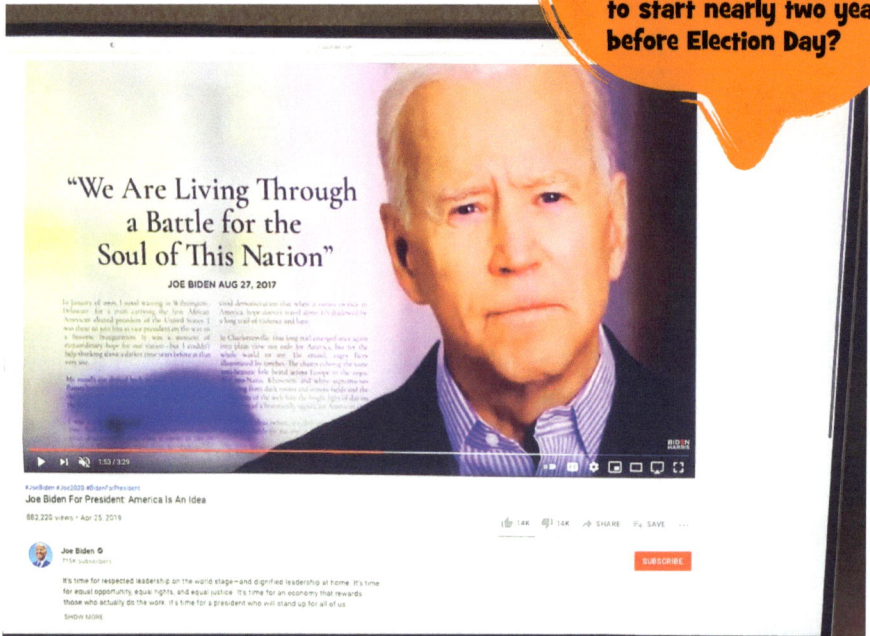

Joe Biden announced his 2020 presidential campaign in a YouTube video.

Candidates hold fundraisers and give speeches during their campaigns.

There can be a lot of candidates in the running early on. Candidates come from all backgrounds. Some of them currently work in politics. They may be serving as senators or governors, for example. Sometimes, candidates are business owners or activitsts. Candidates often spend a lot of time and money to reach voters. They run ads and host events. Candidates talk about the issues they want to fix. They also talk about the plans they have for the country.

Candidates begin to drop out of the race as time goes on. Sometimes, they see that their chances of winning are not very high. So, there is no point in continuing. Other times, they can't afford to keep running. It can cost a lot of money to campaign. Presidential campaigns cost millions of dollars. Candidates need plenty of donations to keep moving forward. They also need a lot of supporters. As the race continues, the **field** shrinks as candidates drop from the race.

Primaries

As campaigns continue, candidates keep hosting events and giving speeches. They meet with voters. They answer questions. They give their opinions on key issues. These issues can divide people. Even within one family, people can and do disagree. That's okay! People have their own beliefs. Voters often choose candidates whose beliefs line up with theirs.

Candidates often travel across the country to meet their supporters.

Caucuses

Some states hold caucuses instead of primaries. These are closed meetings that people belonging to the same political party go to. Caucuses are not as simple as primaries, and they can take a lot longer. Voters listen to supporters, debate issues, and finally make their choices. The delegates they pick go to the national convention. Republican and Democratic caucuses are different.

As the election nears, states hold **primaries**. In the primary elections, each voter chooses their top candidate. The winner of a primary becomes the party's nominee for president from that state.

There are two types of primaries: open and closed. In open primaries, voters can vote for any candidate. In closed primaries, voters can only vote within their own party. Imagine a voter is **registered** as a Republican. But they want to vote for a Democrat. In a closed primary, the voter cannot vote that way. They can only vote for a Republican.

There are pros and cons to both types of primaries. Nearly half of the states have open primaries. In some of the states, the primaries are closed. In others, states let the parties decide which type to have.

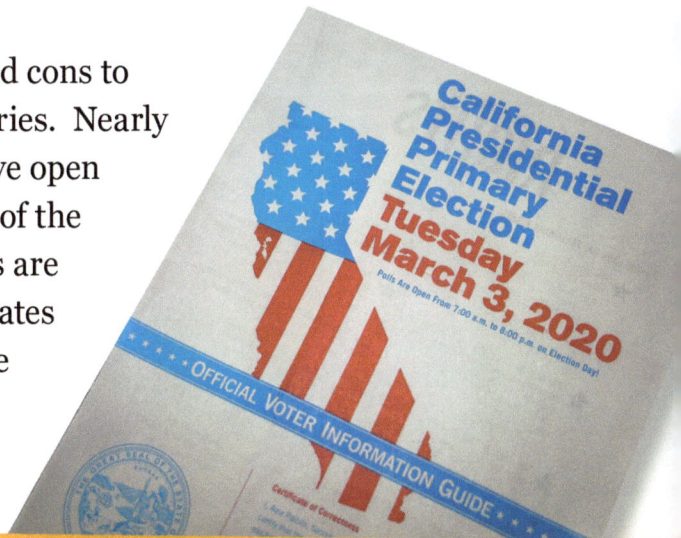

National Conventions

As Election Day nears, voters start to make decisions. They choose who they want to win. But sometimes, the person a voter wants drops out of the race. When that happens, voters have to think again. They study the candidates who are left. They choose someone new.

Every summer before Election Day, each major party holds a national convention. These conventions are large meetings. The party members come together. Here, the party announces its nominee for president. This person won against all other candidates in the party. They won the most votes in the primaries and caucuses. The candidate will be on the **ballot** in November.

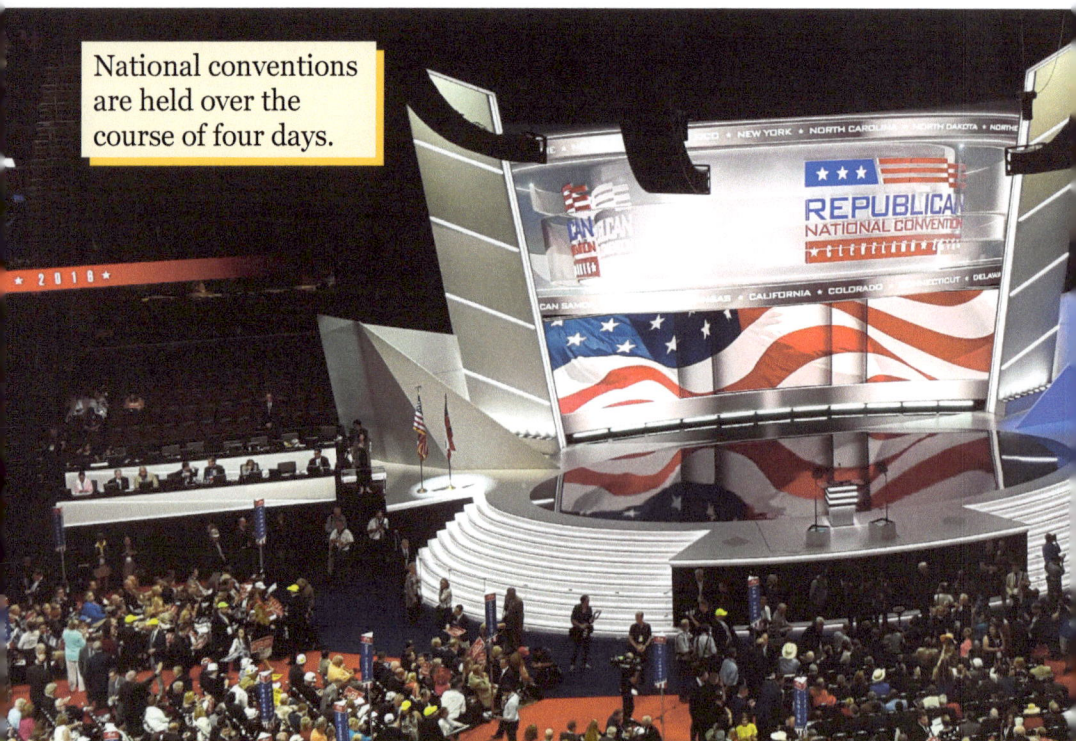

National conventions are held over the course of four days.

Woman of Many Firsts

Kamala Harris was elected as Joe Biden's vice president in 2020. She is the first woman to have this position. She is also the first Black person and Asian American to have this position.

The nominee gives a big speech. People from all over the country come to watch in person, or they watch on TV or online. At this time, the nominee announces their running mate. This person is the nominee for vice president. From this point forward, the two run together as a team.

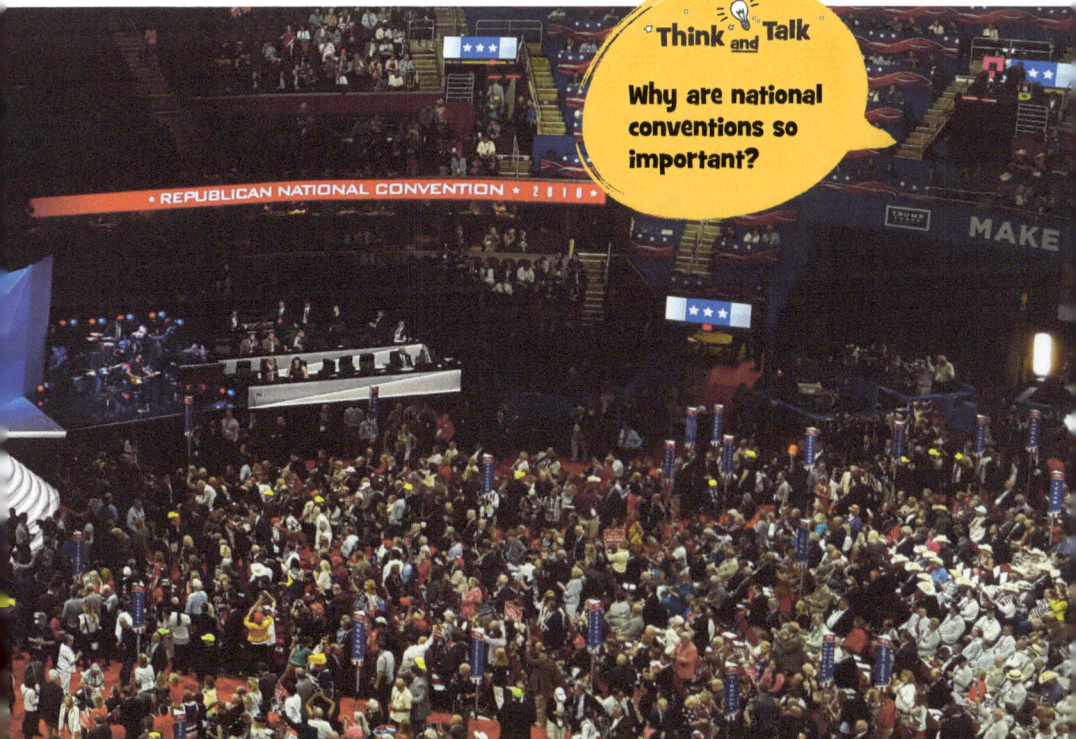

Think and Talk

Why are national conventions so important?

Debates and Election Day

In the weeks before Election Day, the nominees take part in **debates** on key issues. The debates are broadcast through all **media**. The presidential nominees debate. The vice presidential nominees debate as well.

By this point, a lot of voters have already made up their minds about their votes. But some voters still do not know who they want to be president. They are called *undecided voters*. Debates are meant to help undecided voters. Many voters watch them carefully. They compare and contrast the nominees. Watching the debates can help voters make their final decisions.

Bill Clinton (left), George H. W. Bush (center), and Ross Perot (right) at their last debate in 1992

Get Out and Vote

Election Day is held on the first Tuesday after the first Monday in November. Some states consider Election Day to be a holiday. Schools may close. Workers may get the day off. Leaders in these states think that more people will vote if they have more time to do so. Some people vote before Election Day by mail.

Vote by Mail

Leaders in some states think that voting by mail helps to get more people to vote. Voting in person is not always easy. Some people's polling places are far away. Sometimes, there are lines people must wait in for hours to vote.

electronic ballot

For people who vote in person, polling places open early all over the country. Polling places are where voters gather to cast their votes. These places can get crowded. Lines may be long. Voters must be patient.

When people show up to vote, they must be registered. In some states, you can register to vote and vote on the same day. Volunteers tell voters where to go to cast their votes. Some states have paper ballots that voters write on or mark in some way. After voters are done, they turn in their ballots. Some states have computers where people vote digitally.

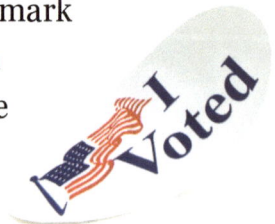

The Final Tally

Once the polls close, the votes are in! People want to know right away who the next president is. But the Framers did not want to use only the popular vote to elect the president. Remember the Electoral College? The Framers had to compromise. That means that the last step of the election can take a while.

Voters choose who they want to win. But in reality, voters are not voting for that person. They're really voting for which **elector** they want to represent their state. Each state has a certain number of electors. The electors cast the votes that elect the president.

The Electoral College

The number of electors equals the number of each state's members in Congress. There are 535 members of Congress. And, there are 538 electoral votes. The extra 3 votes represent Washington, DC. States with more people have more electors. States with smaller populations have fewer electors.

Electors meet in December of the election year. They confirm their state's nominee. Then, they cast their electoral votes for that person. In January, Congress counts the votes from the electors. Nominees must get more than half the 538 electors to vote for them to win the presidency. It is only after this count that a winner is official. Soon after, the new president is sworn into office.

This map shows the number of electors in each state.

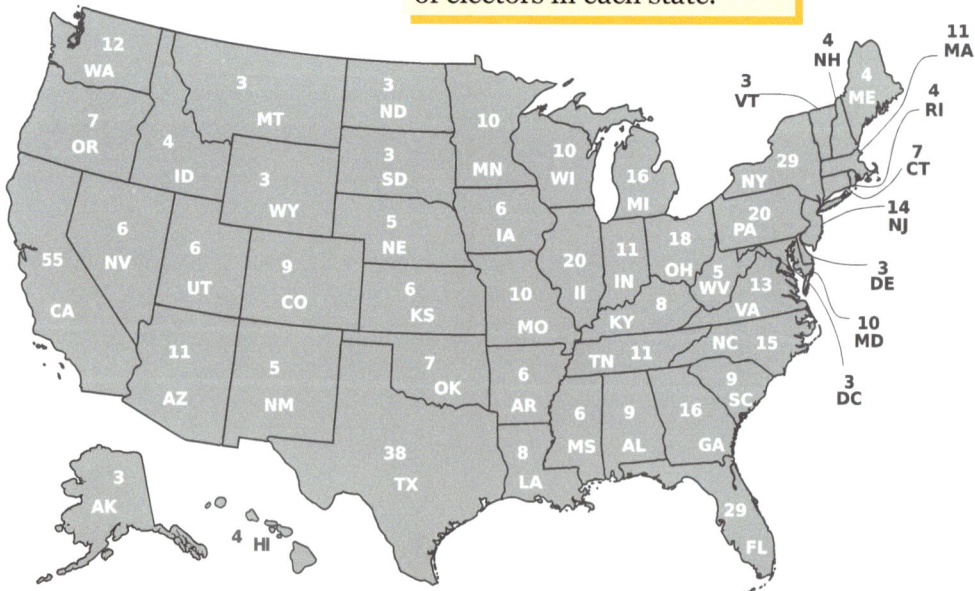

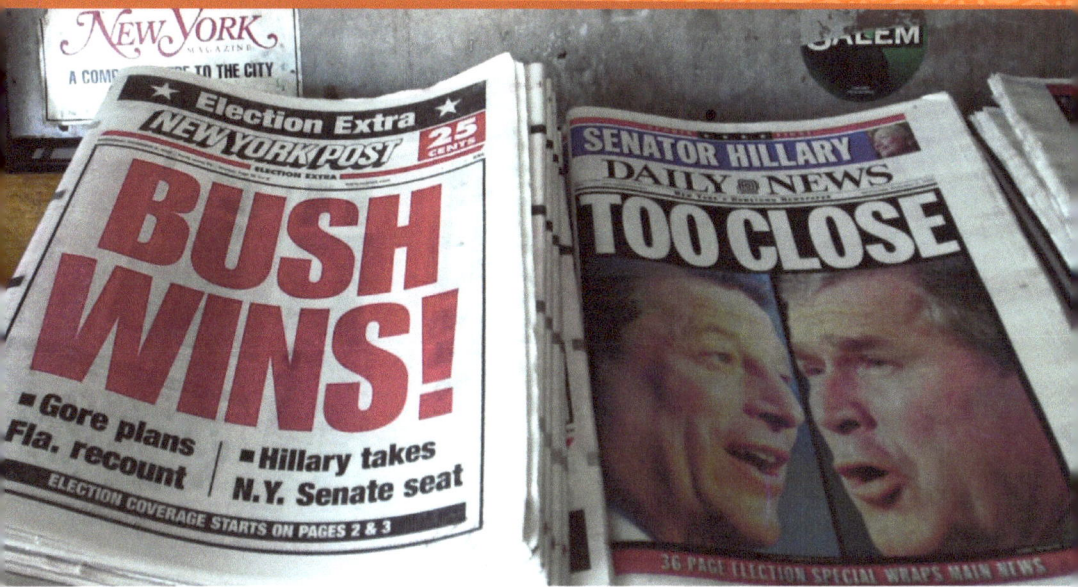

Because the Electoral College chooses the winner, some voters may feel like their votes don't matter. But that is not the case! A few votes can make a huge difference. This was true in the 2000 election. Al Gore was ahead in a close race. News reports called him the winner. But when Florida's votes were counted, George W. Bush had won the state. It was a very close call. Less than 600 votes separated the two nominees in that state.

Small Amount

The 2000 election in Florida was decided by hundreds of votes. Because the vote was so close, Florida law required the votes to be recounted. The winner would be granted 25 electoral votes. The recount took 36 days. The U.S. Supreme Court even got involved. Finally, the numbers confirmed that Bush won. Bush had only 537 more votes in Florida than Gore.

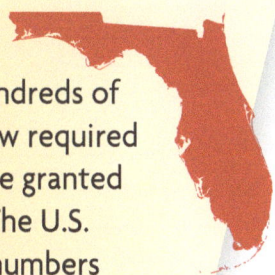

Every Vote Counts!

Although citizens have to be 18 to vote, there are ways for anyone to get involved in the election process. Anyone can watch the conventions and debates. Anyone can also watch the **inauguration** in January. Some children even go with their parents to polling places.

Barack Obama at his 2009 inauguration

People don't have to vote for the president to take part in an election process. Students can vote in their school's student council elections. Families may vote on what to have for dinner. Children might have a say in what to do over the weekend. In these situations, people vote for the option they think is the best choice. In a presidential election, they can still share their ideas with others even if they cannot vote. They can still tell candidates what they think.

No matter the election, votes count! In the United States, adult citizens have a say in who should lead the nation. This has not always been true. People have worked hard to make this happen. The people have earned the right and the responsibility to vote. Close elections continue to prove that each vote makes a difference.

Glossary

amendments—changes to the U.S. Constitution

ballot—a sheet of paper or a ticket that is used to vote in elections

campaign—a series of events political candidates participate in, attempting to win an election

candidates—people who run in elections

citizens—people who legally belong to a country and have its rights and protections

compromise—an agreement made where each side gives up something

debates—formal discussions between candidates where they discuss their opinions and plans on key issues

democracy—a form of government in which people vote for their leaders

elector—a member of the Electoral College

excluded—left out or not included in something

field—the group of people who are in an election, political race, or other contest

Framers—the people who wrote the Constitution of the United States

inauguration—a ceremony to mark the beginning of a new presidency

media—the system of communication through which information is spread to a large number of people, including through TV, internet, and radio

political party—a group that organizes to direct or influence the government

popular vote—a democratic vote for a U.S. presidential candidate made by qualified voters

primaries—elections in which members of a political party nominate candidates for presidential elections

registered—enrolled in an official list to show which political group a person belongs to

Index

Civics in Action

Elected officials work for the people. They need to know about things that are on people's minds. This way, they can work to solve problems. Reading letters is one way to learn what is happening. Plan and write a letter to an elected official.

1. Identify a problem. It may be in your school or community. It may be in the state or even the nation.

2. Explain why this problem is important.

3. Explain how this problem affects people.

4. Identify an elected official to whom you will write your letter.

5. Write and send your letter.

www.ingramcontent.com/pod-product-compliance
Lightning Source LLC
Chambersburg PA
CBHW040932030426
42336CB00001B/12